SIMPLE BLESSINGS

SIMPLE BLESSINGS

Living with a glass half-full perspective

JOE PRUETT

Pruett Books

Author Introduction

My name is Joe Pruett and I am ever so blessed to get to share this book with you. I am a lifelong resident of Conway, Ark. I am a retired insurance agent with AAA Insurance, serving the Conway area for over 35 years. During this time, blessings came my way almost daily in the service I was able to provide to our insureds. I am also a Lay Pastor at Grace Presbyterian Church in Conway, Ark. Growing and serving God is indeed one of life's many blessings I receive.

God has blessed me with a wonderful marriage, two amazing children and five wonderful grandchildren. All blessings in my life, indeed.

I hope as you explore these different blessings you will see just how we are all blessed with the Simple things in our lives. My wish for you is truly for you to live focusing on your blessings and when you do I believe God will make himself even more visible to you in your life. Thank you for allowing me into your life, may we all live reflecting on our many "Simple Blessings".

Joe Pruett

FOREWORD

"Simple Blessings" is a message from my heart to yours. Many of the chapters allow me to share small parts of my life, and you may wonder why this is important. In the big scheme of things it probably isn't since I don't offer you solutions to the deep mysteries of life. Instead, my goal is giving you a sense of how blessed we are regardless of the struggles we face each day. Think of this book as binoculars that help you see the good things that occur in your life; things which may, in turn, help you live with a "glass half full" approach to life.

My background allows me to speak to those of you who are content with your lives, but also to those who feel you are hanging by a thread. If the latter describes you, keep reading, for I believe you will find reasons to enjoy life to its fullest.

One of my favorite holiday movies is "White Christmas" starring Bing Crosby and Rosemary Clooney. My wife and I watch this movie every Christmas as part of our holiday traditions. In the movie there is a scene in which the two stars sit together late at night in a cozy lodge in front of a warm fire. Rosemary tells Bing that she's having trouble sleeping and he responds by singing these words.

"If you're worried and you can't sleep, count your blessings instead of sheep and you'll fall asleep counting your blessings. When my bankroll is getting small, I think of when I had none at all and I fall asleep counting my blessings."

Friends, it is my sincere hope that having read this book, you will come to recognize your blessings, naming them one by one. I think you will discover that life is full of "Simple Blessings"!

I

Blessed Through Goals

Goals: "an aim or desired result; something you are trying to do or achieve"

I find that having goals brings joy into my life as I strive for and, ultimately, achieve them. Years ago, I decided I wanted to live a healthier life, so I set a goal of running in a marathon. Wait! That's 26.2 miles! Who was I kidding?!

At first it seemed impossible. After all, I'm not particularly gifted as an athlete. But when I realized that my only competition would be myself, it began to seem possible. Of course, there are elite athletes who run competitively, but I, like most runners, just wanted to pit myself against myself.

Over time, by setting incremental goals I have been able to run several marathons and half marathons and still find them to be very satisfying. I have met my goal and it has proved to be a blessing in my life.

As you consider setting a goal, take into consideration these guidelines:

1. Be sure your goal is realistic. You don't want to set yourself up to fail.
2. Decide what small goals will help you reach that ultimate goal.
3. Write it down. That step is vital! Don't take it lightly.
4. Tell someone you are setting the goal, and ask them to help you stay on target. This should be someone you see often and admire so you are reluctant to disappoint them. Give them permission to ask you periodically how you are doing in pursuit of your goal.

Seeing yourself completing the smaller goals leading up to your primary goal will give you satisfaction as you draw closer and closer to the "big one". Each step is progress.

Think of something you would really like to see happen in your life. Maybe you'd like to:

- Become debt free
- Learn to play an instrument
- Pursue a new hobby
- Volunteer with a worthy organization

The possibilities are endless and exciting! As you being your journey, watch for moments of success and happiness your efforts bring. Those are blessings! Enjoy them!

Devotional Thought

"Be strong therefore, and let not your hands be weak; for your work shall be rewarded."

2 Chronicles 15:7

When you set a goal and follow the steps necessary for completion, you will be blessed by goals.

2

Blessed Through Family

Family: "the basic unit in society, traditionally consisting of two parents rearing their children"

It's been said that you can choose your friends, but you don't get to choose your family. That means that while there are lots of people who say they came from a wonderful family and have many wonderful memories of their childhood, there are many others who have no memories of their families at all.

I fall somewhere in the middle of that description since I had many trials in my life as a child and young person. But when I married, my wife and I determined to cultivate close relationships within our family. I say determined because different personalities occurring within families sometimes make that a challenge. Commitment to love at all times is essential.

Our relationships grow and prosper when we invest time in those we love. Find time to watch your grandchildren play. Find ways to make them laugh. Listen to them. They can teach us a lot if we slow down and enjoy living in the moment with them.

Our individual stresses diminish as we eat, laugh, and visit with our families. Don't take your relationships with family for granted. Cultivate them! Enjoy them! They are rich blessings in our lives.

Devotional Thought

"Look at how good and pleasing it is when families live together as one." Psalm 133:1

It is our joy to provide for and nurture our families, for this is the will of God. Express your love to your family every day. They are among God's richest blessings.

3

Blessed Through Faith

Faith: "complete trust or confidence in someone or something"

When I was 45 years old, I walked by my pastor's office and said, "Wow! What a great gig you have. You have to work only one hour a week!" Obviously, I said this in jest since I knew there is much more to pastoring than preparing a weekly sermon. As I was enjoying my joke, he continued. "You, my friend, get to enjoy that hour soon because I'm going on vacation during the week of July 4."

That was my first invitation to preach, and it took me three months to write that first sermon! But it was a life-changing experience that led me into training to become a Lay Pastor.

In the Presbyterian Church, a Lay Pastor is one who has received formalized training, but not the full-blown seminary training that allows one to be called an Ordained Pastor. I knew I wanted to pursue that training.

"Strength to Love" is a book which compiles 15 sermons by Dr. Martin Luther King, Jr. For me, it was a life-changing book. In the sermon on faith, Dr. King makes the statement that "Faith is like taking the first step when you don't see the staircase." Please make this book part of your personal library; you won't regret it.

Every day we place our faith in many things. We drive having faith that others will obey the rules of safe driving. We take medications prescribed by our doctors. We have faith our food is safe. But the faith I am referring to is the faith I have in Jesus Christ, my Lord and Savior.

My faith is in my certainty that Jesus Christ died for my sins, rose from the dead and now sits at the right hand of God the Father in heaven. I believe He created heaven and earth and is capable of leading me daily. I trust His words to guide me. I pray that you have that same faith. In a world full of misery, sickness and death it is comforting to know that we can trust God with whatever comes into our lives because He is our Rock and our Redeemer. Faith allows us to step out onto the first step, not even seeing the staircase yet knowing it is there. We are in God's hands.

Devotional Thought

"For we walk by faith, not by sight." 2 Corinthians 5:7

Faith is trusting in things we cannot see. Faith is knowing that God is in control. Release your life to Him and let His love carry you today.

4

Blessed Through Pets

Pets: "a domestic or tamed animal kept for companionship or pleasure"

I love my pets! Psalm 147:9 tells us that God is concerned for all His creation and that has to include his animals. He provides food for the cattle and for the young ravens when they call.

Gary Kurz has written a wonderful book entitled "Cold Noses at the Pearly Gates". In it, he uses scripture to help us understand that our pets live eternally in heaven. I believe pets are one of the ways God blesses us. Pets teach us to live by the way they live. They are loyal, dedicated, consistent, and protective. They model many of the traits we should develop in our own lives.

Our family has always been fond of dachshunds, and we've had at least one in our family for many years. Our first one was named Sparky, and he was a Christmas present to our young children. When Sparky was about 9 years old, he developed a problem with a disc in his back. We took him to Dr. Larry Nafe who was the best specialist in our state. He assured us that surgery would fix the problem and Sparky would be as good as new.

Dr. Nafe performed the surgery and when we picked him up we were given a vet bill of $1200! That was in 1998 and it was a tidy sum. Later, as I was lying on the floor playing with Sparky I said aloud to him, "Boy, did we ever trick Dr. Nafe! We would have paid a lot more than $1200 to have you well!"

It's hard to explain the bond we have with our pets. I wrote a sermon titled "The Faith of Walt". In the sermon, I noted how our dog, Walt, demonstrates complete faith in us. He has faith that we will care for him and love him. That is the faith we can have in our "Owner" Jesus Christ.

Mr. Bill Barry is a retired, single man living alone who has turned his backyard in Arkansas into a pet haven. He has set up cameras, and sends his friends daily photos and videos of all the animals he cares for in his yard as he feeds them daily. He has names for all the animals. Limper is a little deer with a limp, Freda is a fox that comes to his back door for scraps.

Bill has a giving heart and his giving is met with the blessing of grateful animals that come to his backyard. Bill, thank you for caring for these animals, and for sharing this joy with me and many others.

Friends, look on your pets as blessings right at your feet. Observe and enjoy them as you love and care for them each day.

Devotional Thought

"A righteous man regards the life of his animal." Proverbs 12:10

Our pets give us more than we give them. They teach us how to love one another and how to rely on God, trusting him with all our hearts just as they trust us to care for them.

5

Blessed Through Attitude

Attitude: "a settled way of thinking or feeling about someone or something, typically one that is reflected in a person's behavior"

Years ago, I heard Zig Ziglar make a statement which has had a significant impact on my life. He said, "Your attitude will determine your altitude." Over the years I have continued to think about this quote and to apply it to my life. My first employer put this on coffee mugs for us so we could entertain that thought as we began each day.

One's attitude is a good barometer if he wants to know how a day is going to progress. In a sense, we make a day whatever we choose to make it by the way we are thinking. My natural bent is to look at life as a glass half full, so adding my understanding of the power of attitude contributes to my positive attitude.

Every day we encounter situations which threaten our attitudes, and it is our response to the situations that determines the amount of stress we experience. For example, if you find you are often anxious and hurried, you are causing unnecessary strain on your body. If getting to appointments is a typically stressful situation for you, start planning to be there 10 minutes early. While I realize unexpected things still can happen, I think you will find that your life, in general, will be less stressful. You are captain of your own ship and you are in charge of the attitude you harbor.

There is a helpful book by John Mark Comer called "The Ruthless Elimination of Hurry". If you are looking for help in this area, I highly recommend this book. Slowing down is difficult for some of us Type A people, but it is necessary because living a hectic life takes its toll eventually.

Having a positive attitude is contagious. You probably can think of times you have been in a group of people who are speaking negatively and other times when the group is speaking positively. The difference is palatable. You have that power to influence others with your positive attitude, and your stress level will drop in accordance with the way you are thinking.

Anxiety is a killer. I Peter 5:7 says, "Cast all your cares on God for He cares for you." Let this verse be a guiding light for you. Find joy in carrying a positive attitude with you wherever you go, and you will discover that your good attitude produces good altitude. Here's wishing you a HIGH flight!

Devotional Thought

"Finally, brethren, whatsoever things are true, whatsoever things are honest, whatsoever things are just, whatsoever things are pure, whatsoever things are lovely, whatsoever things are of good report: if there be any virtue, and if there be any praise, think on these things." Philippians 4:8

Let your attitude help you live each day joyfully, giving yourself to others with a positive attitude.

6

⬯

Blessed Through Gratitude

Gratitude: "the quality of being thankful; readiness to show appreciation for and to return kindness"

In Chapter Five we established that one's attitude determines one's altitude. Now let's consider the subject of gratitude. It is here that we will discover wonderful secrets about our blessings.

Since you are reading this book, I can safely say that you can be grateful for the ability to read. Are you aware that there are 32 million people in the United States who cannot read?

As I write this chapter today the temperature outside is 22 degrees. But tonight, I will sleep in a warm home unlike the 553,742 homeless people who live in America. You will doubtless experience the same comfort. And it's likely that the food you had for dinner was far superior to the food available to them. Having a warm place to live and good food to eat is certainly a blessing we can acknowledge.

The international poverty line is $1.90 per day, or $693 per year. The average income in the United States is $31,133 per year. So, from an international perspective, we are considered extremely wealthy. Still, it's easy to dwell on what we don't have instead of being grateful for what we do have.

Do you have family and friends? Be grateful for them and for opportunities to share good times with them.

We live in a society that bombards us with definitions of success and fulfillment which sometimes cause us to feel dissatisfied with our lives. But gratefulness doesn't spring from the world's wisdom. Romans 12:2 says "Do not be conformed to this world, but be transformed by the renewal of your mind......." Instead of chasing illusive happiness according to the world's standard, allow your mind to focus on the myriad of things for which you can be grateful. Your thoughts will bless you!

If you can get your hands on a copy of Mike Huckabee's book, "A Simple Christmas" I would encourage you to do so. Mr. Huckabee was governor of the state of Arkansas and ran for U. S. president in 2008, but prior to all of this he was a Baptist minister. His book will lift your spirit as he describes the gratitude he feels for all the blessings God has given him.

Perhaps today you will be able to say thanks to people in your life who are a blessing to you. They will appreciate it and your own gratitude will soar.

Devotional Thought

"In everything give thanks: for this is the will of God in Christ Jesus concerning you."

I Thessalonians 5:18

Express your gratitude to God for the life He has given you. Your life in like no other life, and God designed it just for you. Be grateful for it.

7

Blessed Through Giving

Giving: "providing love or emotional support; caring"

I know you've heard the phrase "It is more blessed to give than to receive." Perhaps you even joked about it saying "Wow, is that ever wrong!" But having experienced the deep joy of giving we know that it is true.

In early 2021, I attended an event where I encountered a gentleman for whom those words are more than a pretty quote. They are a part of his life. The event I am speaking about was a half marathon at the Woolly Hollow State Park in Arkansas. This 13.1 mile run was done on trails through this scenic park which was breathtaking in its beauty.

Prior to our starting the run, the race director took time to pray for all of the participants, and when he completed his prayer, he said, "Folks, the money we raise here today goes to help the needy in Honduras." As he continued to speak it became clear that he has a passion in his heart for the people of Honduras and their needs. But he went further to challenge us to search our hearts to find what we are passionate about and to begin giving to those organizations.

When we think of giving, we automatically think of money, and you may not have much money to give. But money is just one of the things we can give along with time, prayer, or another pair of hands.

- Is your passion to help the needy? Contact The Salvation Army in your area, your local food bank organizations, Habitat for Humanity, or any number of churches in your area that feed the poor.
- Is your passion to help those who are addicted and fighting to find their way in life? Contact rescue ministries in your area and find out how you can assist them in their process.
- Is your passion to help animals? Reach out to humane societies in your area to see how you can assist them with time or money.
- Do you feel passionate about the homeless? Contact appropriate organizations in your area and see how you can help them.

Devotional Thought

"Give, and it shall be given unto you; good measure, pressed down, and shaken together, and running over, shall men give into your bosom. For with the same measure that ye mete withal it shall be measured to you again." Luke 6:38

Live your life focused on giving and watch how blessed you are as a result. No matter how much the world tells us to keep what is ours, it is impossible to out give God. Remember the statement spoken by Anne Frank: "No one has ever become poor by giving."

Winston Churchill once said, "We make a living by what we get; we make a life by what we give." Live every day experiencing the blessings that come through giving.

8

Blessed Through Character

Character: "the mental and moral qualities distinctive to an individual"

When you hear that a man is "a person of character", do you think of that as a positive characteristic? If someone said, "That Joe is such a character!" would you know whether that was a positive or negative assessment? It would become clearer if the statement were "Did you see Joe's actions? He is a person with little character!" No doubt this is a negative statement about Joe.

Sometimes people cannot hear what we are saying because our actions are speaking louder than our words. The definition at the beginning of this chapter uses the words "moral qualities". Our actions or inactions can impact the evaluation of our character, so if we want to maintain a reputation for being a person of character, we must live a life that can bear scrutiny.

Moral quality is also depicted in how we treat other people. We should always seek to build them up and never try to tear them down. This is pleasing to God, as well, for as Pastor Rick Warren has said, "People are interested by talent, but God is impressed by character."

Live your life guarding your character. Blessings will follow.

<u>Devotional Thought</u>

"He that walks uprightly walks surely; but he that perverts his ways shall be known."

Proverbs 10:9

Your character defines you. Live your life so that no one questions your morals. We may not be able to control everything that happens in our lives, but we can respond with character.

9

Blessed Through Courtesy

Courtesy: "having good manners and respect for others"

Let me tell you about a young man I met during a golf tournament in my home town, Conway, Arkansas. Corey is 27 years old and serves our country in the Navy. During the 3-hour competition, I was impressed time and time again with his behavior which was like a breath of fresh air. He answered my questions with a "Yes, sir" "No, sir" or "thank you". I assumed the Navy had played a role in his respectful tone. Corey's father was playing in the tournament, as well, and I mentioned Corey's demeanor to him expressing how enjoyable it was to be in his presence. His dad gave credit to the Navy but went on to say that Corey's high school football coaches also had played a role in Corey's life.

Our conversation brought back memories of my son's days playing sports in the Conway area and I began to recall coaches who helped mold my son in positive ways. He played for some of the same coaches Corey played for, many of whom are still coaching today, still having a positive impact on the students they train.

Courtesy includes doing good things for others with no expectation of a reciprocal response. This life of loving and giving puts a positive stamp on our relationships with other people. This is especially true in our relationships with young people who cross our paths.

Remember to be kind and courteous to others. Psalm 19:14 says "Let the words of my mouth and the meditation (thoughts) of my heart be acceptable in Your sight, O Lord, my Rock and my Redeemer." If we think courteous thoughts, our actions will follow. Let's focus our minds on thoughts of kindness and goodness, of gentleness and peace, remembering that Jesus admonished us to love our neighbors as we love ourselves.

Devotional Thought

"Finally, be ye all of one mind, having compassion one for another, love as brethren, be pitiful, be courteous." I Peter 3:8

Begin today to look for ways to be courteous and kind to others and see how dramatically this blesses your life.

10

Blessed Through Exercise

Exercise: "activity requiring physical effort, carried out to sustain or improve health and fitness"

I get a great deal of enjoyment from running! I like knowing that I am doing something that will improve my overall health. This morning as my wife and I ran, the temperature was a brisk 26 degrees with very little wind and an abundance of sunshine. The conditions were PERFECT!

As we ran, we met a good friend who was running in the opposite direction so we turned and ran a few miles with our friend. As lifelong residents in our community our friends often see us running (not very fast but moving along) and tell us they can see the enjoyment we experience when we run. Simply running is a blessing in itself.

Sharing a life of running and exercising with friends takes the joy to a new level. Through the years I have run miles and miles with people who have welcomed me into their lives and allowed me to welcome them into my life as we spent time together doing what we each love to do.

I encourage you to grab a friend, lace up your shoes and be blessed through exercise. The benefits for your body and for your soul are too numerous to count.

Devotional Thought

"A wise man is strong; yea, a man of knowledge increases strength." Proverbs 24:5

Take time to exercise and nurture your body, treating it as a gift from our Creator. The physical and mental benefits are immense.

11

Blessed Through Memories

Memories: "a recollection of something that happened in the past"

With the exception of one year, I have lived my entire life in the same town. That may sound like a boring life to some people, but for some people like me, change is not a necessary ingredient in a happy life. While our memories are not dependent on living in a specific place, I enjoy reliving some of my memories with my grand-children as I show them where I went to school, or the playgrounds I spent hours on when I was their age. I still recall the drive-in my grandparents took me to when I was growing up. I can still picture the marquis in front of Dog and Suds as though I saw it yesterday.

Let me ask you a few questions. Who were your childhood friends? What is your most memorable childhood experience? Did you play sports in high school, and do you have memories which bring a smile to you lips as you recall them?

Take time frequently to walk down memory lane and remember the pleasant people and events that blessed your life. Do it with a friend who has some of those same shared memories. Even the recollection of reliving those memories with a friend with be an additional blessing in the future.

Devotional Thought

"The memory of the righteous is a blessing...." Proverbs 10:7

God provides us with "pictures of our past" to allow us instant access to the significant moments in our lives. Never take those memories for granted. Cherish them, and know that your blessings are the result of loving others and sharing life with them. Perhaps something that occurs in your life today will bring a smile to your face in the years to come.

12

Blessed Through Love

Love: "an intense feeling of deep affection"

This definition expresses the love I have for others in my life. While there are a number of things I enjoy such as a good movie, a nice dinner, golf, a long run, none of these things measure up to the definition I shared. But when I talk about sharing time with my wife, playing with my grandchildren, and worshipping at church, I am talking about things that I have a deep affection for. In other words, these are things I love.

As a lay pastor I can't think of love without thinking about how the apostle Paul described it. Love is patient and kind. It doesn't envy or boast. It isn't proud. It doesn't dishonor others. It's not self-seeking or easily angered; it doesn't hold grudges. Love does not delight in evil, but rejoices with the truth. It always protects, trusts, hopes, perseveres, and it never fails.

Those are wonderful guidelines for how we should live, especially as we apply them to those closest to us. I am blessed to be married to a woman who exhibits these traits daily and she makes me want to be a better person.

Think about these guidelines as you interact with people this week. Showing love to someone will bless you as well as them.

Devotional Thought

"Love.... does not behave itself unseemly, seeks not her own, is not easily provoked, thinks no evil." I Corinthians 13:5

When Jesus was asked, "What is the greatest commandment?" he said, "Love the Lord with all your heart, soul and mind. The second is to love your neighbor as you love yourself." Always strive to love others as you love yourself. Be patient and kind and look for opportunities to lift up others and you'll find yourself lifted, as well.

13

Blessed Through Kindness

Kindness: "the quality of being friendly, generous and considerate"

We are blessed through the kindness we show to others and by the kindness they show to us. It's a win-win situation. What does it mean to be kind? Kindness is an attitude of the heart. A heart that is kind is always willing to give help when needed. It consistently expresses itself with goodwill toward others.

For many years I was blessed to work next to a person who was one of the kindest people I had ever known. His kindness was inspiring to me; I wanted to learn to be more kind myself. When we are kind to someone else, the action affects us as well. We are blessed as much as they are.

Here are some examples of how we can show kindness to another.

- Slow down when driving.
- Call a friend to see how they are doing.

27

- Take a meal to someone or invite someone to have a meal with you.
- Take the trash can down for a neighbor.
- Mow a yard for an elderly person.
- Be patient.

Kindness is a virtue that lifts the spirit of the giver and the recipient. Be kind!

Devotional Thought
"Be kindly affectionate one to another with brotherly love; in honor preferring one another.
Romans 12:10
Let your life be defined by kindness. Look for ways to be kind, for kindness heals and strengthens others. A life lived with kindness is a life well lived.

14

Blessed Through Mentors

Mentors: "to advise or train someone, especially a younger colleague"

Throughout my life I have been blessed to have wonderful mentors. From a very young age I have been associated with men of character who have advised me regarding many facets of my life. I am not speaking of educational training; I am speaking of life training. These men have patiently used their own experiences to guide me as they shared knowledge and direction with me which would not have been available to me otherwise.

A true mentor is able to hear your concerns and give you wisdom gleaned from his or her experience. That input is incredibly helpful because it is realistic and pertinent. Now that I am in my late 50's, I find myself in the role of mentor and what others have taught me is proving very beneficial as I try to help others.

Has there been someone in your life who has helped you along life's journey? Have you expressed your thanks to them for helping you as you have traveled? Is there someone in your circle who would benefit from a mentor? Are you that someone?

Hebrews 13:16 says "Do not forget to do good and to share with others, for with such sacrifices God is pleased."

Devotional Thought

"As iron sharpens iron, so one person sharpens another." Proverbs 27:17

It is likely that there are people in your life who have no one to show them the things that you could teach them. Be willing to use your time and knowledge to mentor another person.

15

Blessed Through Confidence

Confidence: "the feeling or belief that one can rely on someone or something; firm trust"

We face many decisions every day, some easy, some difficult. The ones we face easily are the ones where experience has given us confidence that we are doing the right thing. Years ago I was the pastor of a small church in a small town, and every week I prepared a sermon for the people in my congregation. In the beginning, it was somewhat difficult because I was new to the preaching ministry, but week by week I began to notice that it became easier and I began to develop confidence in my ability to prepare the sermons.

Have you noticed that many famous people, especially those with athletic prowess seem to carry themselves with an air of confidence? There's a word that's used to designate a few of these elite performers. GOAT stands for "greatest of all time". When you hear the names Jack Nicklaus, Tiger Woods, Hank Aaron, Tom Brady, or Michael Jordan you can readily see how apt the word GOAT is. These players displayed time and time again the ability to deliver under pressure. They demonstrate the value of confidence. One doesn't have to be the greatest at anything to be blessed by confidence. But it does take patience and effort to develop skill on a higher level and that development is rewarding.

I've said a lot about how much I love running, but I have never won a race. I'm simply was not fast enough to have win any of the races I have entered. BUT, I have finished every race I have ever run. That gives me confidence that I will be able to complete whatever task I attempt. Live your life confident in your relationship with God. Confidence is not arrogance or pride but rather strength that comes from above

Devotional Thought

"So do not throw away your confidence; it will be richly rewarded. You need to persevere so that when you have done the will of God, you will receive what he has promised."

Hebrews 10:35-36

Live your life knowing that when you have made a commitment and prepared yourself for it you will be blessed through the confidence that follows!

16

Blessed Through
Forgiveness

Forgiveness: "the action of releasing resentment for an offence"

Forgiveness can be given or received, and they are both essential for your mental, physical and spiritual health. My first sermon was entitled "Forgiveness – It Will Set You Free". When we forgive others, we are freed from the burden of carrying anger inside ourselves.

A wonderful example of forgiveness is recorded in a book called "Unbroken" which tells the story of Louis Zamperini who was a prison of war in Japan during World War II. The book highlights the incomprehensible treatment that he and other soldiers received at the hands of their captors. The forgiveness Louis demonstrated is a lesson to all of us regarding the beauty of forgiveness.

Dr. Martin Luther King said "Forgiveness is not an occasional act; it is a permanent attitude". Determine always to forgive the offenses that come your way and you will be blessed. If that has not been true of you in the past, begin today to make that commitment. Carrying grudges, anger, and resentment will remove blessings from your life. The softest pillow is a guilt free conscience. When you learn to forgive, your life will be blessed beyond measure.

Is there someone you need to forgive right now? I promise that if you will do you will find blessing in that action. One of my favorite authors, Max Lucado, said "The key to forgiving is to quit focusing on what someone did to you and start focusing on what God did for you.",

Devotional Thought

"And be ye kind one to another, tenderhearted, forgiving one another even as God for Christ's sake hath forgiven you." Ephesians 4:32

Forgiveness sets you free to embrace life like never before. Remove the heavy chains of grudges and forgive others as you have been forgiven.

17

Blessed Through Perseverance

Perseverance: "continued effort to do or achieve something despite difficulties"

Life is full of obstacles, and perseverance is essential as we face various trials. Learning how to remain steadfast regardless of the difficulties one faces is learned through perseverance. The culture in which we live is quick to define winning as "finishing first", but sometimes the blessing comes in somehow finding the way to persevere when difficulties arise.

One real life example of this perseverance was displayed in the 1984 Summer Olympic games held in Los Angeles. That year was the first year for the running of the Women's Marathon Race. Obviously, every runner in that race was trying to win a medal for being the first to complete the marathon. But it is possible that the biggest winner in that competition was Gabriela Anderson-Scheiss who did not finish first. Gabriela finished thirty-seventh of 44 runners in the race.

But here is the story behind the story. The rules for this raced allowed only 5 water aid stations on the course. The temperature was mid to upper 80's, and the importance of staying hydrated can't be overstated. Sadly, Gabriela missed the last of the 5 water stations which left her in a very dehydrated condition. As she entered the stadium 20 minutes behind the winner, she was all alone and the crowd in the stadium and hundreds more watching on national TV gasped as she staggered onto the track. Her torso was twisted, her left arm limp, her right leg seized. She waived away medical personnel who rushed to help, knowing that if she were touched by another person she would be immediately disqualified from the race. The crowd stood and cheered as she made the last lap in the stadium. That lap, which normally would have taken her less than one minute, took over 5 minutes due to her condition.

Gabriela personified the word perseverance that day. So, no matter what difficulties or trials you face, remain persistent to the end and you will be blessed through perseverance.

Devotional Thought

"And let us not be weary in well doing; for in due season we shall reap, if we faint not."

Galatians 6:9

The secret to living with the changes each of us faces every day is to trust God and say, "I can keep alert and persevere no matter what may come my way."

18

Blessed Through Anniversaries

Anniversaries: "the date on which an event took place in a previous year"

What special events do you celebrate? If you are married, you probably celebrate your anniversary every year. And you probably celebrate your birthday. Other events which are special to you are also worthy of a celebration. Some time ago, the church I was attending celebrated their 100th anniversary with all sorts of special events. I recall writing a letter that was put into a time capsule which will be dug up and read in 2092. High school reunions are often celebrated at 10, 20, 30, and even 50-year anniversaries. Many find enjoyment in reconnecting with high school friends after many years apart.

Some anniversaries involve life altering events such as those experienced by men I teach at Renewal Ranch. They celebrate anniversaries of their sobriety as they recover from their addictions. They are blessed as each anniversary extends their length of abstinence. All of us are blessed through anniversaries. Cherish those anniversaries and pause to remember the blessings associated with them.

Devotional Thought

"His sons used to go and hold a feast in the house of each one on his day, and they would send and invite their three sisters to eat and drink with them." Job 1:4

Relationships that include love and honor for another person are bound to succeed. Let your love shine so that others will know how much they mean to you. Watch this grow year to year as you celebrate the anniversaries in your life.

19

Blessed Through Patience

Patience: "the capacity to accept or tolerate delay, trouble, or suffering without getting angry or upset"

Oh, what a wonderful word to explore! How do you deal with delays? Delays are a common day experience and the way we navigate through them has a huge impact on our lives. Learning to live at a slower pace is necessary for a calm, peaceful life and it will help us deal with delays.

Just driving across town can give us ample opportunities to practice our patience. Sometimes it seems every red light catches us as we hurry along. If ever we needed patience, it's when we're driving.

In the summer of 2021, we saw an Olympic athlete who had to endure with patience. Simone Biles, arguably the greatest female gymnast of our time, had to withdraw from several events due to issues with her mental health. Having trained for years and years, she must have been incredibly disappointed in her inability to participate. But we watched Ms. Biles stay strong as she competed in one of the final events. She has learned patience.

Patience can help you overcome the trials, disappointments and struggles you face. Determining to be patient causes us to rely on others and, ultimately, to rely more fully on God. His plan for our lives is more fully accomplished when we implement Psalm 46:10 which says, "Be still and know that I am God." This is His directive to us as we face the vicissitudes of life. I pray you will find strength to endure when facing troubles and live patiently one day at a time.

Devotional Thought

"With all lowliness and meekness, with long suffering, forbear one another in love."

Ephesians 4:2

Patience is a virtue which promotes kindness, gentleness and sincerity toward others. These are the fruits of living patiently.

20

Blessed Through Helping

Helping: "to make it easier for someone to do something by offering one's services or resources"

Helping others is an amazing and fruitful experience. I have a friend who embodies this topic to its fullest. His name is Ed Powers. Ed and his wife Sondra both are in their uppers 70's, and when they moved into our town, we found them to be an amazing couple. They were high school sweethearts and they have been married for 57 years. A few years ago Ed's wife had a stroke which necessitated some changes in her life, but she and Ed have not let this slow them down. Knowing them makes this chapter easy to write.

Ed is his wife's caregiver, and while some might think this is a burden on Ed, I can tell you that this is not the case. The amazing thing is that in addition to caring for his lovely wife, Ed cares for so many others, as well. Let me remind you again that I stated he is in his upper 70's! A couple of weeks ago he got up on the top of his neighbor's roof to blow off the leaves. He also mows lawns for some of his other neighbors. He does all this while lovingly caring for his wife. I don't have earthly heroes, but if I did I can assure you the sacrificial love I see displayed in Ed would put him at the top my list.

I don't spend a lot of time on social media, but today I saw this on the Facebook page of a fellow church member. Her page popped up with a photo of an elderly lady sitting at a table with a young man around 20 years old. The caption said he was merely asking if he could share a meal with her and enjoy the time together. What a beautiful way to bless another person!

Have you ever been at a drive thru restaurant and pulled up to pay only to learn that your order had been paid for by the car in front of you? Have you ever done this for another? If not, try it sometime. Just pull up to McDonald's and pay for the meal for the person behind you. I suspect there will be two people leaving with a joyful heart. Take a cue from my friend Ed, who has learned the art of helping others. I suspect you will find increased joy and happiness in your own life.

Devotional Thought

"Bear one another's burdens, and so fulfill the law of Christ." Galatians 6:2

Take a moment to help another in need. This does not have to be a long, drawn-out event. It could be as simple as a phone call to a lonely friend. Look for opportunities to help someone else.

21

Blessed Through Mercy

Mercy: "compassion or forgiveness shown to someone whom it is within one's power to punish or harm"

In our next two chapters, we will discuss mercy and grace. Our definition above makes it easy to connect this to our relationship with God because we receive his mercy every day. God's grace is seen as He shows us compassion and forgives us for the sins we commit. But they are also vitally important to us in our relationships with each other.

Initially, when I think of mercy in our society, it is easy to connect this with our judicial system. Daily, people appear before judges who weigh the facts of the case and determine whether mercy is merited or punishment is due. The circumstances of each case have a bearing on the decision.

One day on my way to work, I approached a railroad track. At that very moment, the lights on the bars started blinking and the bars started to lower. I hurried across the tracks. I could see there were no trains nearby, but with the bar lowering, I should have stopped and waited. A policeman coming toward me saw all of this occur and immediately pulled me over. He was kind and considerate, and I was guilty of going when I should have stopped. His first words were, "Why in the world did you do that?" I had no acceptable reply except to say that I had made a mistake in judgment. At that point he could have given me a citation, and it would have been deserved, but he chose to use this as a teaching lesson and gave me a warning and suggested that I refrain from doing it again in the future.

Mercy taught me never to make that same decision again. Can you think of a time when you were given mercy? Can you see that you got something you did not deserve? Even more importantly, when have you shown mercy to another? We all are in a position in our lives to give mercy to others, even to those whom you might consider to be your enemies. It is easy for us to stand on a pedestal and demand that justice be given, but to take the higher road and offer compassion and forgiveness is a sign of a Godly heart and soul; it is a wonderful way to live.

Today, look for ways to show mercy to someone. This could be as simple as a warning from a police officer or the forgiveness of a worker in a drive thru who has omitted part of your order. Live being blessed by the mercy you give as well as the mercy you have received.

Devotional Thought

"Be ye therefore merciful, as your Father also is merciful." Luke 6:36

God has shown mercy to us; we must pass that mercy along to others. We are never more like Him than when we are merciful to others.

22

Blessed Through Grace

Grace: "a generous, free and totally unmerited and undeserved gift"

In our previous chapter we touched on the idea of mercy, and I stated that we would connect this with the word grace. As a lay pastor, I frequently share the benefits we have received from Christ. One of these benefits is a perfect example of our definition, for as believers, we have received a free and unmerited gift from God. Grace frees us in many ways. Since we have been forgiven we can see the importance of forgiving others who have harmed us in some way. What joy there is looking at others in the light of their goodness and not in the light of the trespasses they have committed.

Earlier I mentioned Max Lucado who is one of my favorite authors. In his book, "In the Grip of Grace", he points out that sometimes we find ourselves comparing our lives to others. He gives a wonderful analogy that demonstrates the fallacy of such comparisons. Let's say, for a moment, that God put out an order that said the only thing any of us has to do to reach heaven is to jump to the moon. That's it. Just reach down and jump up and touch the moon. Some might actually try to do it and they might jump 4 feet or even higher. That's much higher than I can jump, so compared to me, they would be much closer to reaching the moon and heaven. However, when compared to the distance of the required jump, which is 238,900 miles, even our greatest attempts would never allow us to make it. We simply cannot earn it by our jumping ability.

God's grace is a free gift. Attempting to pay for it renders it no long free. Take a moment to reflect on your life. Have you ever offered grace to another? You may be surprised at how often you do this as you give to others without expecting anything in return. This is living a grace

filled life. Determine to enjoy the grace you have received and give that grace to others.

Devotional Thought

"Let your speech always be gracious, seasoned with salt, so that you may know how you ought to answer each person." Colossians 4:6

God loves us so much that he gives us grace upon grace, removing our sins because of His Son Who carried them to the cross. We did not earn this, cannot pay for this, and can never do anything to be worthy of it. But that is what makes it GRACE! Live in peace because of the free gift God has given to you.

23

Blessed Through Struggles

Struggle: "a forceful or violent effort to get free of restraint or conviction; to fight, grapple, or wrestle"

In prior chapters I have shared with you a number of books which have been a blessing to me. The truth is that we are blessed simply because we can read! I will continue to tell you about books which have had an impact on my life.

Our very lives are perilous and, as the old saying goes, we are all just a phone call or breathe away from being on our knees. I believe God uses struggles in our life to not only strengthen our tie to Him, but also to allow us to comfort others in their difficulties. In his book, "Beating Goliath", Art Briles tells his story about football and his faith. Coach Briles was one of the most successful coaches in the history of Texas high school football and then went on to be very successful in the college ranks, as well. His story is unique. When he was in college, his parents and another very close friend died in a car wreck on the way to watch him play football. His life took a turn in that instant. Coach Briles explains the impact of the accident on his life, and then tells how he gained an ability to help others through this trial.

God used a tragic event in his life for good in the lives of others. While we want and hope that things will just simply go according to a plan, unforeseen things happen. But struggles, disappointments and trials do not have to define who we are; we can use these events to build our strength. You've probably heard the statement that you are either coming out of a struggle, currently in one, or soon to be headed toward one because life is full of ups and downs.

Instead of letting your trials define who you are, let your faith in God bring you through them knowing that He will walk beside you all the way. Trials can bring growth as you learn more fully how to trust God and count on His help. Isaiah 41:10 is a wonderful verse to memorize. It says, "So do not fear, for I am with you; do not be dismayed, for I am your God. I will strengthen you and help you; I will uphold you with my righteous right hand." As you grow, share your experiences with others. Your story will encourage and bless them.

Devotional Thought

"Be strong and courageous. Do not be frightened, and do not be dismayed, for the Lord God is with you wherever you go." Joshua 1:9

Our struggles give us the chance to see God in action, lifting us up and giving us hope in the face of trying times. Always remember you are never alone when you trust in God and lean on Him for guidance.

24

Blessed Through Vacations

Vacations: "an extended period of leisure and recreation, especially one spent away from home or in traveling"

Our lives are so hectic and busy that sometimes we just need to take a break. Vacations offer us the opportunity to stop and smell the roses and to reflect on our lives without the distractions of life. As you read this chapter, I want to encourage you to recall the places that have brought you joy as you visited them.

Personally, Walt Disney World is that place for me and my family. You might guess that when I tell you that our family pets are named Walt and Disney! Each of the trips we have taken there has left us with special memories. The trips originally began many years ago with my little family, meaning my wife, myself and our small children, our little family has now grown into a family of eleven, including grandchildren, who love these "magical memories" at Disney World.

Sometimes when people bump into folks they know when they are on a trip, they say, "It's a small world, isn't it?!" One of our favorite rides is "It's a small, small world". You might even be humming the tune to the song as you read these words.

We need to be mindful of the rest and energy we can derive from taking a well needed vacation. You will be blessed by the memories you make.

Devotional Thought

"Come to me, all ye who labor and are heavy laden, and I will give you rest." Matthew 11:28

Our bodies were not meant to run at full speed all the time. Slow down and see how blessed you are through vacations.

25

Blessed Through Trust

Trust: "a firm belief in the reliability, truth, ability or strength of someone or something"

Take a look at one of coins in your pocket and you will see the words "In God We Trust". The inscription has appeared on most U.S. coins since the Civil War. They were inscribed there to serve as a constant reminder that the nation's political and economic fortunes were tied to its spiritual faith. The idea of trusting in something larger than ourselves can bring comfort to us.

When you make an agreement with someone, whether it is verbal or written, can that person trust that you will do what you say you will do? Trust is a difficult thing to reinstate once it has been broken. Marriages often are destroyed by lack of trust when one partner makes a poor decision that leads to disaster for the family. But when two individuals are able to maintain their trust in each other, the blessings are immense. In the past, it was not un-common for men to shake hands on an agreement knowing that the handshake was all that was needed to insure trust. That transaction spawned the phrase "my word is my bond."

Prior to retiring, I sold insurance for a living. Individuals who sign a policy with an agent count on his company to provide the services the policy outlines as they are needed. If this fails to occur, the client's lack of trust will cause the company to lose him as a client. Other consequences may occur, as well. While we cannot control every aspect of our lives, maintaining our integrity is one thing we can control. When you say that you will do something for someone, make your word your bond and keep the promise you have made. This will solidify their trust in you and bless you in innumerable ways.

When you become a person who can be trusted, people will turn to you for help. Be careful to maintain your good name and try to help those who come to you for advice or help. I mentioned earlier about marriage and well this is the ultimate in the line of trust. Live today and everyday seeing the blessings of trust in your life.

Devotional Thought

"Trust in the Lord with all your heart, and do not lean on your understanding." Proverbs 3:5

Live each day trusting God to guide your steps. He will lead you down the proper paths if you will follow his lead. Your trusting him begins by accepting his Son as Lord and Savior of your life. You can choose to go it all alone or you can trust in the creator to guide you. My friend, trust in God!

26

Blessed Through Reading

Reading: "to discover information in a written or printed source"

Reading opens a world of information on any topic that interests us, and our options are varied and accessible. The idea of writing this book, "Simple Blessings" came to me while I was reading a book. The previous year I had written a weekly editorial article for our local newspaper that enabled me to share ways in which my readers could discover blessings in their everyday lives. Many other authors do the same thing weekly, each having his/her on insight on a variety of different subjects. There is much we can learn from the written experiences and expertise of other writers.

I have not always had a passion for reading, but at about the age of 45, the desire to read and learn exploded in my mind! Since that time I've enjoyed many, many books and articles. If reading has not been a part of your life, know that it is never too late to begin. I know you will be blessed by what you learn and experience by reading.

I have shared the names of many books for you to consider

adding to your reading list. My hope is that you will discover the blessings associated with picking up a book or newspaper as you begin your own reading journey. Here is a list of other books and authors I think you will enjoy.

Dr. Martin Luther King, Jr. "Strength to Love"

John Mark Comer "The Ruthless Elimination of Hurry"

John Ortberg "When the Game is Over, All the Pieces Go Back in the Box"

Jimmy Buffett "A Pirate Looks at 50"

Eric Blehm "Fearless, the Adam Brown Story"

Brandon Webb "Among Heroes"

James Patterson "The Christmas Wedding"

Admiral James Stavridis "Sailing True North"

Any book by Max Lucado and John Grisham

By all means spend time with God and His word. You will find that reading brings richness to your life. An exciting world is waiting for you to explore through reading.

Devotional Thought

"Study to shew thyself approved unto God, a workman that needs not to be ashamed, rightly dividing the word of truth." 2 Timothy 2:15

When we read, we gain knowledge that is useful to ourselves and helpful to others as we pass this knowledge along. Let your reading of God's word be a priority as you seek to grow spiritually and to guide others in your sphere of influence.

27

Blessed Through Hope

Hope: "a feeling of expectation and a desire for a certain thing to happen; a feeling of trust"

What are you hoping for at this time of your life? For many in our city, state and nation, there is the hope for good health to return to our lives. The pandemic we've been experience for the last two years has left some people feel hopeless. Others are hoping for a new marriage, a child birth, a new career opportunity, or a host of other things. Hope gives us something to look forward to.

A recent study reports that the three things a person needs most are: someone to love, somewhere to go, and a feeling of HOPE! It really makes sense doesn't it? Having someone to love, who returns that love, is a beautiful gift. Having somewhere to go is also part of the excitement of living. When you plan a vacation, you hope for good weather, safe travels, and fun along the way.

I heard a wonderful sermon recently in which our pastor gave this amazing analogy. He related that in New York City one can do down to 5th Avenue and see the statue of the strong man holding the world over his head. He reminded us of how the strong man seems to be struggling to carry the weight of the world on his shoulders. Our pastor said if we walked across the street, we could go into a church parish where there is a statue of Jesus as a young boy comfortably holding the world in His hand.

Hope involves trust. Where are you placing your hope as you deal with the difficulties of life? Are you handing them off to the strong men of the world, who are struggling with their might to uphold it? Or, are you putting your life in the hands of Jesus, who loves and cares for you? I encourage you to let Jesus fill you with hope every day.

Devotional Thought

"For I know the plans I have for you, declared the Lord, plans for welfare and not for evil, to give you a future and a hope." Jeremiah 29:11

Our hope is found in living daily with God. Let your life be guided by His glorious hand for He has plans for all His children and those plans are to give you a future and HOPE.

28

Blessed Through Joy

Joy: "an inner feeling, it endures hardships and trials and connects with meaning and purpose"

It is easy to confuse happiness and joy. Happiness is an outward expression. One can pursue happiness, but joy is an inner feeling of the heart. I have a deep sense of happiness in my life because of the love my wife has shown to me for the past 40 years. But what we experience in our relationship goes beyond happiness. It is an immense inner feeling of joy that comes from knowing that our love is strong and true.

A few weeks ago at church, we sang "Joy to the World". Before we sang the carol, one of our song leaders, Mr. Don Bingham, provided some history on this song. He said that while many think of this song as merely a Christmas song, it was actually written to be sung all year long. The lyrics speak of the joy that is ours because Jesus came into the world.

I read an article in "Compassion, Inc," which offered these insights into the concept of joy. Joy is in the heart. Joy is of the soul.

Joy goes beyond the limits of something. Joy embraces peace and contentment, waiting to be discovered. Joy is a practice and a behavior, it is deliberate and intentional. A person chooses joy. Joy is profound and scriptural.

When we read and study the Bible we find that God resides in our hearts. That is His domain, and out of our hearts flow our thoughts and emotions, our inner workings.

Devotional Thought

"Count it all joy, my brothers, when you meet trials of various kinds, for you know that the testing of your faith produces steadfastness." James 1:2-3

Joy can be found in the minute-by-minute moments in our lives as we walk with a loved one, enjoy a sunset, or watch a sleeping child. None of our material things bring that deep sense of joy. Decide to live your life joyfully.

29

Blessed Through Peace

Peace: "freedom from disturbance; tranquility"

Many aspects of life threaten our peace. Conflicts and tensions seem to be ever present. It is the awareness of this lack of peace that has driven me to write this book. My goal has been to open our eyes to the blessings we might not be aware of which can make our lives more peaceful and content. When asked, "What is the greatest commandment?" Jesus said the greatest commandment was to love God with all our hearts and then to love our neighbors as ourselves. To love another like we love ourselves takes the meaning of an "other centered life" to a new level.

Peace flows to us when we speak to others as we want to be spoken to, consider others as we would like to be considered and live with love in our hearts for others. Self-centeredness comes much more easily because it is our natural bent. Take a look at any young child and you will see how possessive they are with their toys and other belongings. However, as we mature physically and also in our walk with Christ, we are better able to lay aside our own wants and desires and focus on the needs of others.

The Hebrew word for peace, Shalom, has a much richer connotation than the English words conveys. It carries the idea that peace is more than the absence of conflict; it implies that a blessing is attached to that peace. It conveys the notion of a positive blessing, especially in terms of a right relationship with God that results in the assurance that all is well. When we live our lives rightly related to our creator, we find peace that surpasses all understanding.

Devotional Thought

Isaiah 26:3 "You will keep him in perfect peace whose mind is stayed on You because he trusts in You."

God doesn't want you to simply have peace in your life; He wants you to have perfect peace. Allow your mind and heart commune with God. If you find yourself wandering away from Him, go back home to perfect peace. Shalom.

30

Blessed Through Friends

Friends: "a person with whom one has a bond of mutual affection"

Have you ever taken a moment to reflect on how much it means to have a mutual affection for another person? Unfortunately, as we age, our circle of friends seems to diminish. This is part of the circle of life as our growing families leave less and less time for us to nurture the friendships we had prior to such growth. Having a special bond with another person is a priceless gift.

I want to point out a few ways you can continue to cultivate and grow these special friendships. First, we must determine to stay in touch with people who are special to us. Failure to communicate will destroy that sense of closeness. Our lives are busy, but if we value our friendships, we will take the time to stay in touch with them.

Second, we need to be sensitive and compassionate. Many of us have friends who are having a difficult time dealing with the changes that are occurring in their lives. Initiating a contact with them lets them know that we are available and care about their needs. Your call will help them and it will bless you, as well.

The bonds that you nurture will stay with you through the years, and your long term friends will be a continuing source of blessing to you and to them. Begin today to strengthen and build on your friendships and discover the blessing they bring to your life.

Devotional Thought

"A friend loves at all times, and a brother is born for adversity." Proverbs 17:7

Live your life mindful of the joys God has given to you in your association with others. Don't take friendships for granted; invest time in those who are dear to you.

31

⟨❧⟩

Blessed Through Purpose

Purpose: "the reason or purpose for which something is done or created"

I am blessed to share my life with men at Renewal Ranch. This Christ based facility is helping addicted men get their lives back on track by showing them how a relationship with Christ can help them overcome their addictions. One of the tools I use to help them is a book by Rick Warren called, "The Purpose Driven Life". At times, we need help in defining our purpose in life, and Pastor Warren put together a wonderful book to guide us in our journey.

In the final chapter of my book, I want to share with you Pastor Warren's steps for determining one's purpose.

1. You were created for God's pleasure. Learn what makes God smile, what is at the heart of worship, and how to become best friends with God.
2. We were formed for God's family. We are Gods children and He cares for us a father lovingly cares for his children.

3. You were created to become Christ like. In this step we learn what transforms us and what tempts us, and how we can defeat those temptations.

4. We were shaped for serving God. We learn how to use what God has given us, how we act like real servants.

5. We were made for a mission. We learn how to share our life message, how to become a world class Christian and how to live with a purpose.

Understanding our purpose will guide us as we make choices that will restore us.

Devotional Thought

"For I know the thoughts I think toward you, says the Lord, thoughts of peace and not of evil, to give you an expected end." Jeremiah 29:11

Living a life without a purpose is like a sailing a ship at sea without a rudder. A life lived in this manner is like drifting with no idea of the intended destination. God created a plan for you. Seek to know and follow God's special plan for your life. When you goal is to honor Him, your perception of your life will become clearer each day.

CONCLUSION

My hope for you, dear reader is that the ideas I have expressed in this book will help you focus on the many blessings you have in your life. No one has the prefect life, and that includes the richest man on this earth and those who are struggling from paycheck to paycheck. Often times, when we live with an abundance of things it is easy to lose sight of some of the best things in our lives. Please don't let this happen to you. Live with your eyes open to all the beauty and glory that is all around you. Be aware of the children in your life who bring you such joy. These are part of God's blessing to you.

I remember asking a good friend of mine why he chose to become a pediatrician, and he told me it was because children do not want to be sick. Children want to play, and play and play some more. We need to be more childlike in our perception of life, understanding how God continues to bring good things into our lives for our joy and delight. He wants us to live trusting Him and enjoying the lives He has given us.

The Lord bless you and keep you; the Lord make His face shine upon you, and be gracious to you; the Lord lift up His countenance upon you, and give you peace.

ACKNOWLEGEMENTS

No project can be completed without the help of others. This statement is especially true regarding the effort that went into the preparation of this book. I must say Thank You to a number of individuals.

First, thanks to Ms. Jeannette Stewart at the Log Cabin Democrat for allowing me to submit weekly articles to your newspaper in 2021. Without you, I suspect this book never would have materialized.

Thanks to Ken Johnson and Chuck Seifert for being the best "mentors" a person could have. You are much more to me than mentors; you are like fathers. Thank you for caring and teaching me many things about life.

Thanks to Eloise Stowe for editing and choosing the right words to express the ideas I longed to share with others.

Thanks to the readers of the Log Cabin Democrat who corresponded with me. Your kind words regarding my articles gave me confidence to embark on this book; I hope you enjoy it.

And last, thanks to my loving wife. You show me how to live "others centered". I am convinced that God put you into my life to teach me so I could share with others. You are my greatest blessing from God.

CPSIA information can be obtained
at www.ICGtesting.com
Printed in the USA
LVHW081150130422
715961LV00009B/482